Unique Pets

Madagascar Hissing Cockroaches

Kristin Petrie

ABDO Publishing Company

visit us at
www.abdopublishing.com

Published by ABDO Publishing Company, PO Box 398166, Minneapolis, MN 55439.
Copyright © 2013 by Abdo Consulting Group, Inc. International copyrights reserved in all
countries. No part of this book may be reproduced in any form without written permission from the
publisher. The Checkerboard Library™ is a trademark and logo of ABDO Publishing Company.

Printed in the United States of America, North Mankato, Minnesota.
052012
092012

 PRINTED ON RECYCLED PAPER

Cover Photo: Pete Oxford/Minden Pictures/National Geographic Stock
Interior Photos: Alamy pp. 7, 9, 11, 17, 19; AP Images p. 21; iStockphoto p. 15;
    Photo Researchers p. 13; Thinkstock p. 5

Series Coordinator: Megan M. Gunderson
Editors: Megan M. Gunderson, BreAnn Rumsch
Art Direction: Neil Klinepier

Library of Congress Cataloging-in-Publication Data

Petrie, Kristin, 1970-
  Madagascar hissing cockroaches / Kristin Petrie.
      p. cm. -- (Unique pets)
  Includes index.
  ISBN 978-1-61783-441-7
  1. Madagascar hissing cockroach--Juvenile literature. I. Title.
  QL505.7.B4P48 2013
  595.7'28--dc23
                          2012011509

Thinking about a Unique Pet?
*Some communities have laws that regulate the ownership of unique pets. Be sure
to check with your local authorities before buying one of these special animals.*

CONTENTS

MADAGASCAR HISSING COCKROACHES

What insect hisses like a snake, fights like a ram, and acts in movies? It's the Madagascar hissing cockroach! That's right, this sinister-looking insect is a movie star! Its frightful hiss makes it perfect for scary movies. Yet, its gentle nature allows even the youngest actors to handle it.

The Madagascar hissing cockroach belongs to the family Blaberidae. Its scientific name is *Gromphadorhina portentosa*. Common names for this interesting insect include giant hissing cockroach and hisser.

These hardy bugs are easy to care for and do not mind being held.

Hissers are popular pets around the world. Why? Though large for insects, they make compact, easy-going pets. They do not require large cages or special foods. And, their hissing noises are entertaining!

WHERE THEY LIVE

To find a Madagascar hissing cockroach in its natural **habitat**, you'd have to travel to the African island of Madagascar. Madagascar is home to thousands of insect species. Some of these are the largest insects in the world! Many, including the hisser, are island natives.

Why is Madagascar home to so many creepy crawlers? Good question! Insects such as hissers thrive due to the island's climate. Warm, **humid** areas support rapid reproduction. And there is plenty of food, water, and space to keep many creatures comfortable.

In this ideal setting, hissers stay primarily on the rain forest floor. There, debris such as fallen leaves and decaying logs collects. This is where hissers like to make their homes. They are primarily **nocturnal**, so they spend many daylight hours resting in their dim dwellings.

In the wild, hissers may live together in groups.

DEFENSE

This sounds like a nice cushy life, right?
Hissers live in the rain forest and sleep in soft beds
of leaves and decaying stuff. But don't be fooled!
Madagascar hissing cockroaches don't have it so
easy. In the wild, their main job is to be food for
others!

Now who or what would consider a hisser to be a
tasty feast? Many creatures would, as it turns out.
Birds, spiders, ants, and other insects all enjoy a
crunchy roach.

A loud hiss can scare off some hungry enemies.
But, the Madagascar hissing cockroach's best
defense is to hide!

Unfortunately, hissing and hiding cannot
discourage all predators. Humans destroy forests

for agricultural and commercial use. This threatens the hissing cockroach's **habitat**.

THE PET TRADE

Taking hissers from the wild for sale in the pet trade can harm their natural environment. These insects are an important part of their forest habitats. They eat leaf debris and help keep the soil healthy.

Luckily, many Madagascar hissing cockroaches are bred in captivity to be sold as pets. Are these insects allowed as pets in your town? Be sure to do your research before buying one. Then find a responsible breeder, and enjoy your new pet!

Hissers are too slow to simply run away from most predators.

What They Look Like

The Madagascar hissing cockroach looks much like the average cockroach. It has a head, a **thorax**, and an **abdomen**. An **exoskeleton** covers its entire body. This thick, hard, waxy shell is dark brown to black in color.

Two antennae sprout from the roach's head. Three pairs of creepy legs extend from its thorax. And its feet feature pads and hooks that allow hissers to climb most any surface!

But something is missing. Can you guess what it is? Wings! Unlike many of their cockroach cousins, Madagascar hissing cockroaches cannot fly.

At two to four inches (5.1 to 10.2 cm) long, hissers are among the largest cockroaches. They weigh one-fourth to seven-eighths of an ounce (7 to 25 g). Male hissing cockroaches are slightly larger than females.

Males and females differ in other ways, too. Males have heavier, hairier antennae. They also have a pair of bumps or horns called pronatal humps. Females have much smaller bumps.

BEHAVIORS

The Madagascar hissing cockroach's tame manner makes it a good pet. However, in its natural **habitat** this cockroach shows some attitude! Male hissers are **aggressive**, especially when defending their territory.

When their domain is invaded, males use their horns to fight. They also stand on their back legs to show off. Loud hissing adds to this fierce display. In fact, the hisser that hisses loudest usually wins! Female and young Madagascar hissing cockroaches rarely fight.

Hissers can tailor their hisses for specific situations. One hiss sounds an alarm. Another says, "I'm ready to fight!" Yet another between male and female says, "Come on over! I'm ready to mate!"

In the wild, male hissers will defend territory such as a rock for months. They will leave only for food and water.

FOOD

Since Madagascar hissing cockroaches are primarily **nocturnal**, they get busy when darkness falls. What do they do first? Eat, of course!

Madagascar hissing cockroaches are omnivorous, opportunistic feeders. This means they will eat just about anything, wherever and whenever they find it.

In the wild, the Madagascar hissing cockroach's primary food source is decaying plants. This includes rotting trees and leaves, fallen fruit, and other plant matter lying on the forest floor. Hissers even munch on dead animals and insects, too.

Luckily, a pet cockroach does not need a diet of dead and decaying things. It is very happy with pretty much the same things you eat. Oranges, bananas, and peanut butter are tasty favorites. However, many owners simply provide a diet of delicious dog food!

Pet hissers must also have water available. They will suck water from a wet sponge or damp debris in their surroundings.

A hisser's mouthparts are designed for chewing.

REPRODUCTION

After eating, there is more work to be done. What comes next? Babies! Madagascar hissing cockroaches can reproduce after five months of age. Mating can occur year-round. When females are ready to mate, they produce a specific odor. Males detect this scent with their antennae.

After mating, **fertilized** eggs remain in the female's body. Inside the eggs, small **nymphs** develop for about 60 days. Then the eggs hatch, and the mom pushes her squirmy babies out of her body. This gives the appearance of live birth!

Did the mommy hisser have twins? Triplets? No way! Hissing cockroaches produce a whopping 15 to 60 nymphs at a time!

A female hisser can reproduce 30 times during her life.
That means she can have hundreds of babies!

The tiny hissers stick with mom for another five to ten months. During this time, they outgrow their **exoskeletons** and **molt** approximately six times. When they have reached adulthood, it's time to do what hissers do best. Eat and reproduce!

CARE

When should you adopt your adorable six-legged pet? Madagascar hissing cockroaches are so tough they can be adopted at any life stage. However, a newly **molted** roach has a delicate **exoskeleton**. Therefore, handling just after molting is not advised.

Your Madagascar hissing cockroach is easy to care for. Its only requirements are food and water, warmth, and a clean **environment**.

In a dirty home, your pet hisser may acquire mites. These are harmless, but are best avoided in the first place. Timely removal of old food and water and keeping the cage clean will keep the mites away.

Last, handle your hisser with care. Pick it up slowly and gently. Let it walk freely on your hands. Holding hissers down will end up hurting you more than them! The sharp hooks on their legs can catch your skin. Ouch!

Careful handling of your hisser is good for you and your pet!

THINGS THEY NEED

Before buying your Madagascar hissing cockroach, buy its home! A hisser does not need a large home. But, it should be one that does not allow your pet to escape. For this reason, your hisser's home will need a secure lid.

Many owners keep their Madagascar hissing cockroaches in aquariums. Provide wood chips so your **nocturnal** pet has nice bedding and a place to hide from the light. Include cardboard or mesh in the tank for your hisser to climb on.

Tanks kept above 72 degrees Fahrenheit (22°C) will encourage the most activity in your pet

cockroach. Many owners accomplish this with heaters placed under the tank.

Your active, happy Madagascar hissing cockroach will not do tricks or cuddle with you. However, a well cared for hisser can provide years of fascinating sounds and entertainment!

Your Madagascar hissing cockroach may live for up to five years.

GLOSSARY

abdomen - the rear body section of an arthropod, such as an insect or a spider.

aggressive (uh-GREH-sihv) - displaying hostility.

environment - all the surroundings that affect the growth and well-being of a living thing.

exoskeleton - the outer covering or structure that protects an animal, such as an insect.

fertilize - to make fertile. Something that is fertile is capable of growing or developing.

habitat - a place where a living thing is naturally found.

humid - having moisture or dampness in the air.

molt - to shed skin, hair, or feathers and replace with new growth.

nocturnal - active at night.

nymph (NIHMF) - an immature insect.

thorax - the middle body section of an arthropod, such as an insect or a spider.

WEB SITES

To learn more about Madagascar hissing cockroaches, visit ABDO Publishing Company online. Web sites about Madagascar hissing cockroaches are featured on our Book Links page. These links are routinely monitored and updated to provide the most current information available.

www.abdopublishing.com

INDEX